THINGS WILL LOOK BETTER IN THE MORNING

This edition published in 2023
By SJG Publishing, HP22 6NF, UK

Author: Rebecca Dickinson
Cover and text concept design: Milestone Creative
Contents layout: seagulls.net

ISBN: 978-1-913004-62-0

Printed in China

INTRO

What if there was a way to feel happier that didn't involve wine or winning the lottery? A way to experience inner contentment, regardless of what was going on around you? Even when things aren't going our way, there is always something to be positive about. Sometimes it's just a case of knowing where to look.

The good news is that we can all train ourselves to be happier. It doesn't matter where you live, what you look like, what you do for a job, how much you earn or what you've been through in the past; happiness is available to us all. So, let's begin with a little positive psychology.

You might be surprised to learn that only a small amount of the way we feel is determined by the events in our lives.

'There are dark shadows on the earth, but its lights are stronger in the contrast.'

Charles Dickens

In fact, studies suggest that only around 10 per cent of our happiness is contextual – or influenced by the things that happen to us. A further 50 per cent of our overall happiness is thought to be down to our genes, which means there's a whole 40 per cent left to play with. That's a massive chunk of happiness over which we have control.

In case you're thinking 40 per cent doesn't sound like a great deal, think of it this way: it's like the difference between failing or acing an exam; the difference between being healthy or morbidly obese; the difference between a glass half full or a glass half empty. That critical 40 per cent is all that stands between you and a life that flows with joy and fulfilment. And it's there, waiting to be embraced.

Using techniques drawn from positive psychology, and backed up by scientific research, this little book will help you to harness that 40 per cent by developing a more positive mindset. It will guide you towards hope, confidence and resilience. Because whatever your situation, switching to a more optimistic way of thinking can transform your whole outlook on life, leading to a happier, healthier, sunnier you.

As you turn positivity into a habit, other areas of your life will start to improve too. You will feel empowered to take on challenges, overcome difficulties and strive for your goals. Developing a brighter outlook can even have a beneficial effect on your relationships, as well as your physical and mental health.

Within these pages, you'll discover practical tips, uplifting quotations and inspiring ideas to help you see the light at the end of every tunnel and to find joy in every day. However, if you feel consumed by worry or negative thoughts, or if your situation feels so overwhelmingly difficult right now that you are struggling to cope, then put this book down and seek professional help before continuing. Sometimes the first step is asking for help.

'Turn your face toward the sun and the shadows will fall behind you.'

Maori proverb

WHAT IS HAPPINESS?

Happiness means different things to different people. But if there is one thing we can probably all agree on, it's that we would all like more of it. For some people, happiness is associated with possessions or wealth – luxury holidays, expensive clothes, a stylish home. Others might link happiness with success – achieving top marks, getting a promotion or a pay rise at work, clinching a deal, winning an award, or even reaching the dizzy heights of fame and recognition.

'Happiness:
The state of
pleasurable
contentment
of mind; deep
pleasure in or
contentment
with one's
circumstances.'

Oxford English Dictionary

Of course, these things can give us a buzz, but science tells us the effects are short-lived. Researchers have found that when we experience positive events – such as getting married, securing that dream job, or even winning the lottery – we get an initial spike of joy, but after a while we return to our original level of happiness. Psychologists call this the 'hedonic treadmill'. As you get used to your new situation, the novelty wears off. Interestingly, the reverse is also true. So, after going through difficult events, most people will, in time, recover and get back to their baseline state of happiness.

But if happiness isn't determined by the things that happen to us, where does it come from and how do we get more of it? Well, there are two types of happiness. Firstly, there's the pleasure we get from doing stuff that makes us feel good, such as eating a delicious ice cream, buying new shoes or having sex. The feeling that accompanies pleasurable activities is often called 'hedonism', and there's absolutely nothing wrong with this type of happiness. In fact, doing stuff you love (as long as it's safe and legal) is a great way to give your mood a boost. But, as you might have guessed, this type of pleasure is easily swept under the wheels of life. It's lovely while it lasts, but it quickly wears off.

Fortunately, there's another type of happiness that is much longer lasting. It's known as 'eudaimonia' (from the Greek word used to describe happiness). This kind of happiness comes from within; from the deep and meaningful stuff in our lives, the stuff that gives us not just pleasure, but purpose.

We can all experience more of this inner contentment by focusing on qualities like kindness, gratitude and mindfulness, as well as through nurturing our relationships with others and ourselves, and engaging in the things we are passionate about. All this can make an enormous difference to your well-being, resulting in a brighter outlook on life. So, are you ready to choose happy? Then please read on.

'Certain things catch your eye, but pursue only those that capture your heart.'

Ancient Indian proverb

THE PHYSICAL BENEFITS OF LOOKING ON THE BRIGHT SIDE

Happiness is more than just a feeling. Science shows it can have a positive effect on your physical health too. Here are some ways that happiness can improve your health.

You will be doing your heart a favour. Studies have demonstrated a link between happiness and having a healthier heart, including lower blood pressure and a reduced risk of cardiovascular disease and strokes.

You will be more able to cope with stress. When we are stressed, our bodies release the stress hormone cortisol, which can cause health problems, but research shows that people who are happier have less cortisol in their blood.

You will be less likely to become ill. Research also shows that positive emotions can strengthen your immune system, giving you increased protection against illness and infection. For example, in one study, scientists exposed volunteers to the common cold virus. They found that people who reported experiencing more positive emotions were less likely to develop symptoms. Another study exposed people to the hepatitis B vaccine. The results showed that participants with more positive emotions were twice as likely to have a high antibody response.

You will recover faster. We all get sick at some point, but studies suggests that happier people tend to recover faster from illness and surgery.

You will be in a better position to cope with pain. Studies also show that people who are happier tend to have a higher pain threshold and, therefore, experience less pain. This can be especially helpful with chronic conditions such as arthritis.

You will be more likely to live to 100. Ever wondered what the secret of old age is? Research confirms that happier people tend to live longer, which perhaps isn't so surprising, given all the other health benefits.

'Too many people measure how successful they are by how much money they make or the people that they associate with. In my opinion, true success should be measured by how happy you are.'

Richard Branson

BODY POSITIVE

As we have just discovered, positivity doesn't just affect us on the inside; it affects us on the outside too, contributing to a healthier, longer life.

That's because the mind and body are as inseparable as two sides of a coin. You can't ignore one without impacting the other. This means that when you take care of your body, your mental well-being benefits too. We are all aware of the importance of eating well, staying hydrated and trying to fit some activity into our daily lives. But there is one thing that we often skimp on, and that's sleep. However, for things to look better in the morning, we need to start the night before.

THINGS WILL LOOK BETTER AFTER A GOOD NIGHT'S SLEEP

Sleep matters. In fact, it's the single most important way of looking after your physical and mental health. A good night's sleep doesn't just help us to feel energized and refreshed, it provides vital protection against numerous illnesses, including Alzheimer's, diabetes, obesity, heart disease, and many other conditions. Getting a good night's sleep also plays an essential role in memory and learning. But on a day-to-day level, it just makes us feel human and ready to take on the world – or at least our tiny corner of the world.

Most of us need between seven and nine hours sleep per night. However, one in three people have trouble either nodding off or staying asleep. Fortunately, there is a lot we can do to improve our chances of sleeping well. Try to incorporate the following suggestions into your life to help you get a grip on sleep.

Stay regular. Studies show that going to bed and waking up at the same time each day is the best way to help you fall asleep faster and improve the quality of your sleep.

Switch off. Humans have evolved to be active during the day and to sleep when it's dark. As darkness falls, the brain produces the sleep-promoting chemical melatonin. In the morning, sunlight suppresses the production of this chemical so that we wake up naturally. This is called our 'circadian rhythm'. However, in the modern world, this natural 24-hour sleep–wake cycle is disrupted by artificial light. The blue light emitted by screens reduces the production of melatonin, interfering with our ability to fall asleep. Switching off devices at least an hour before going to bed and dimming the lights promotes the natural production of melatonin, setting you up for a much better night.

Call last orders on caffeine. The caffeine contained in tea, coffee and some fizzy drinks can stay in your body for up to eight hours. So, have an afternoon cut-off point of around 2pm and opt for something herbal or milky instead.

Stay off the booze. Although alcohol can help you to relax and fall asleep initially, the effects soon wear off, making you more likely to have a disrupted night. Alcohol also reduces the quality of your sleep as it prevents you from entering deep sleep, meaning you are less likely to wake up feeling refreshed and restored.

Fit some exercise into your day. Exercise has so many benefits, and that includes promoting a better sleep pattern. Research shows that people who do some form of activity during the day tend to fall asleep faster and sleep more soundly. Try to avoid exercising too late in the evening, though, as raising your metabolism too close to bedtime makes it harder to fall asleep.

Keep cool. As your body prepares to sleep, your temperature naturally drops. To encourage this process, keep your bedroom nice and cool. It should also be as dark as possible too, so consider investing in blackout blinds, if necessary.

Keep a pen and notebook handy. If thoughts, worries or crazy ideas have a habit of popping into your head when you're trying to nod off, then having somewhere to write them down is a good way of keeping them quiet until morning. Keep a pen and paper next to your bed so you can note down any rowdy thoughts without having to get up.

'Sleep is that golden chain that ties health and our bodies together.'

Thomas Dekker

Eat earlier. Eating too close to bedtime can mean your body is busy digesting when it's time to settle down, so try to eat at a reasonable hour, when possible. However, avoid going to bed hungry as this won't help you to sleep either!

Get up if you need to. If you've been in bed for what feels like hours without falling asleep, get up and find something calm to do, such as reading. When you start to feel tired and relaxed, go back to bed.

SUPER-CHARGE YOUR MORNING ROUTINE: HOW TO START THE DAY ON A POSITIVE NOTE

Are you the kind of person who pings out of bed with a spring in your step the minute the alarm goes off? Or do you hide under the duvet until the last possible second, before peeling yourself from the mattress and heading straight for the caffeine. Millions of us find it a struggle to get up in the morning. If you're the kind of person who often starts the day feeling groggy and grumpy, you'll know the effects can hang around all day like a bad smell – which is why developing a positive morning routine is so important.

Research suggests that people who get up early have a more positive state of mind than those who go to bed late and sleep in. It might be a struggle at first, especially if you're a natural night creature, but it's worth persevering for the difference it can make to your overall mood. Here are some tips to help you conquer that morning inertia and wake up as you mean to go on.

Get an earlier night. There's no doubt about it, some of us are born night owls. But that doesn't mean you can't switch to become a morning person. It may sound boring, but if you want to wake up refreshed and ready to take on the day, you need to go to bed at a reasonable time. And no, 2am doesn't count! Try shifting your bedtime by just 15 minutes each day, until you're getting around eight hours of sleep. Even if you struggle to fall asleep at first, try to avoid lying in the following morning. Getting up early helps break the cycle. Plus, it will set you up for a positive day, so it's a win-win situation.

Put your alarm clock out of reach. Resist the snooze button at all costs! A few extra minutes under the duvet won't make getting up any easier, so you might as well get it over with. If necessary, move your clock or phone to the other side of the room so you've got no option but to get up to turn it off.

Do a countdown. Still can't drag yourself out of bed? Try counting backwards from five, then jump out of bed. 5, 4, 3, 2, 1 and go!

Keep a bottle of water next to your bed. As soon as you open your eyes, have a glug of water. Great for soothing a dry mouth and kick-starting your metabolism at the same time.

Welcome the light. Fling back the curtains, roll up the blinds or – if it's still dark outside – flick on the lights. The presence of light sends a message to your body to stop producing melatonin, the chemical that helps you sleep.

Think of something that makes you smile. Try to think of at least one thing you're looking forward to, or are grateful for, to inspire you to embrace a new day.

Get some fuel. A good breakfast fuels the day after a night of fasting, helping to boost energy levels, concentration and mood. Don't have time to whizz up a smoothie or fry an omelette? Try overnight oats instead for a ready-to-eat option.

Get a protein fix. Eating some protein in the morning will help keep you energized for longer than eating sugary carbs. Protein also increases the amount of dopamine in your blood, which is associated with motivation as well as pleasure. Protein can be found in loads of foods, including dairy, such as cottage cheese and yoghurt; nuts and seeds; eggs, fish and meat.

Shake a limb. As little as 20 minutes of moderate exercise can boost your mood for the next 12 hours. There's nothing like a brisk dawn walk to help you feel energized and ready to face the day ahead. If that's not possible, then try a quick home workout to get your blood circulating. There are plenty of great videos online.

Notice the difference. If you find it hard to see positive changes on a day-to-day basis, use a journal or tracking app to record your mood. This will allow you to see the bigger picture and can help motivate you to stick to your new routine. Remember, consistency is key.

'Just one small positive thought in the morning can change your whole day.'

Dalai Lama

THINGS WILL LOOK BETTER OUTDOORS

It's not called the 'great outdoors' for nothing. As the pace of life becomes ever faster, and the demands on our time ever more relentless, there is no greater stress relief than getting outdoors.

Our lifestyles are so full of micro-stresses – the morning alarm, the bottomless inbox, the constant ping of our phones – that our brains are in a perpetual state of over-stimulation. Yet immersing ourselves in nature, away from the hustle and bustle of everyday life, allows us to switch off and just be. The simple act of spending time outdoors helps reset the mind and body, and nature offers a 'protective zone' for psychological well-being that goes way beyond the powers of medication.

Research shows that spending time in green spaces lowers blood pressure, reduces muscle tension and decreases the production of stress hormones. One report in the science journal *Nature* revealed that 120 minutes in nature a week lowered stress and boosted the immune system. Other studies have found that people who live close to the sea are significantly less likely to experience mental health problems. That's great if you live near the coast or in the countryside, but what if you don't?

Fortunately, it doesn't matter where you live. The outdoors is all around us, waiting to be embraced. Sometimes we just need to notice it. Even in cities, tuning in to the sounds of birdsong, the sight of new leaves on the trees, the changing sky above the buildings or the rustle of the breeze can lift our mood. So, grab a coat, or slap on some sunscreen, and get some air.

LITTLE WAYS TO CONNECT WITH THE OUTDOORS

- Swap the gym for an outdoor workout or run in the park.

- Walk or cycle to work, or get off the bus a stop earlier and walk the last bit.

- Take your phone calls outside.

- Conduct meetings outdoors.

- Drink your morning coffee outside.

- Eat your lunch in the nearest park or green space.

- Meet friends and family for picnics, walks or bike rides.

- Take up an outdoor hobby, such as gardening or birdwatching.

- Go foraging – but make sure you know what it is before eating it!

- Take your shoes off – feel the grounding effect of the earth beneath your feet.

- Buy yourself a bunch of (sustainably grown) flowers.

- Treat yourself to some houseplants. When you can't get outdoors, indoor plants are the next best thing. As well as being soothing and stylish, they also help to clean the air. Just don't forget to water them – although not too often!

> 'The most difficult thing is the decision to act, the rest is merely tenacity.'
>
> **Amelia Earhart**

THE HAPPINESS DIET: A HEALTHIER WAY OF THINKING

The good news? You can teach yourself to be happier and more positive. The bad news? There's no quick fix.

Let's compare gaining happiness to losing weight for a moment. If you need to shift a few kilos it's no good going on a crash diet – at least, not if you want to keep the weight off. The only way to really lose weight is to adopt a healthy eating plan for life (although, of course, treats are allowed too).

It's the same with happiness. It starts with making a conscious decision to choose positivity or, to use the diet analogy, to switch to a healthier way of thinking. This involves focusing on the way you interpret experiences and questioning your inner narrative. Like any skill, this takes time and practice, but it will help you to become the positive person you want to be, which will empower you to live your best life. Some great qualities that positive people possess can be found on the following page.

'What the eyes see and the ears hear, the mind believes.'

Harry Houdini

1. They are optimistic.

2. They are kind and compassionate.

3. They are enthusiastic.

4. They are productive.

5. They are thankful.

6. They are interested in others and the world.

7. They are self-confident.

8. They are authentic.

9. They are honest.

10. They are adaptable.

11. They are hopeful.

12. They are resilient.

13. They love life.

14. They are fun to be around.

15. They spread joy to others.

GIVE YOUR MIND A MAKEOVER: TOOLS FOR BOOSTING POSITIVITY

If there's one thing happy people have in common, it's that they actively look for the best in any situation. They evaluate events, including negative ones, in ways that are positive and beneficial.

Unhappy people, on the other hand, tend to dwell on the negative. Even in a positive situation, they will focus on the not-so-good bits. As self-destructive as this sounds, there's a biological reason for it. Way back in evolutionary history, our predecessors were programmed to stay alert to physical dangers, such as sabre-toothed tigers. They needed to focus on the negatives in order to stay safe. The trouble is, while life has moved on our brains are still stuck in the Stone Age: our DNA is hard-wired to look for threats.

In extreme circumstances, this piece of mental engineering can come in handy, like if you're about to step off the kerb at the wrong moment. But as most of us don't face life or death situations very often, our unconscious minds project danger on to other stuff instead, so that everyday challenges can feel like sabre-toothed tigers – or oncoming lorries. This is called the 'negativity bias', and it's why we often dwell on unpleasant experiences rather than positive ones. It's as if our brains are stuck on an endless soundtrack of stress and anxiety.

To add insult to injury, we are more likely to attach greater significance to the bad stuff than the good stuff, which explains why you are more likely to ruminate on an insult than bask in a compliment. In other words, even when positive stuff does happen, we tend to miss it. Fortunately, we can override the negativity bias using techniques such as gratitude and mindfulness, which we will come on to shortly. But first, it's important to notice your own thought patterns.

FIRST STEPS TOWARDS OVERCOMING THE NEGATIVITY BIAS

1. **Acknowledge its existence.** Being aware of the way your brain works won't, on its own, stop negative thoughts from occurring, but it will help you to understand why you overreact in certain situations.

2. **Acknowledge when it happens.** Knowing what kind of situations trigger your negativity reflex will help you to prepare for them.

3. **Acknowledge how you feel.** Making the link between your thoughts, behaviour and feelings can motivate you to turn things round for the better.

TIPS FOR CHALLENGING NEGATIVE THINKING

Now that you understand a bit more about how your brain is wired, it's time to address some of those unwelcome thoughts.

Notice when a negative thought pops into your head. Perhaps you're so used to looking on the gloomy side of things that you barely even notice when you're doing it. Recognizing unhelpful thought patterns is the first step towards undoing them. It might help to record negative thoughts in a notebook. This can help you to understand when and why they crop up.

Ask yourself: Does this negative thought have a right to exist? Is there any solid evidence to suggest it's true? Often, you will find there isn't.

Look on the flip side. For example, instead of looking at the things you got wrong, focus on something you got right. In time, this will help shift your awareness from negative to positive.

THE HAPPINESS DIET: A HEALTHIER WAY OF THINKING

Shut it down. Whenever a negative thought rears its head, make a conscious effort to think of something positive. If the negative thought keeps trying to butt in, keep pushing it out. Again. And again.

Ask yourself: What's the worst that can happen?
This may sound counter-productive, but allowing your brain to explore the most ridiculous scenarios can help you to realize how unlikely they are to occur.

Then ask yourself: What's the best that can happen?
Visualizing a situation where things go right – instead of wrong – helps shift your thinking style from pessimistic to optimistic.

Defeat your own worst enemy. Quit being your own biggest critic and telling yourself: "I'm not capable," "I don't deserve that," or "I'm not good enough". This kind of self-talk doesn't serve any purpose; it simply holds you back from following your dreams. Which is one good reason to knock it on the head.

Try being your own cheerleader. When in doubt, tell yourself: "I've got this," or "I am enough". You might not believe it at first – it might even sound silly – but give it a go! And keep going until you believe it. Your mindset is a powerful force, and where your thoughts go, your behaviour will follow.

'Yesterday is not ours to recover, but tomorrow is ours to win or lose.'

Lyndon B. Johnson

LITTLE WAYS TO LIFT YOUR MOOD

It's hard to think negative thoughts when you're doing something fun or pleasurable, so here are a few simple ways to give yourself a boost.

Cuddle a furry friend. Research shows that stroking pets can trigger feel-good hormones and reduce the stress hormone cortisol. If you don't have a cuddly creature of your own, perhaps you could borrow one from a friend.

Have a clear out. Being surrounded by clutter can raise your cortisol levels. So, pick a drawer, corner or even a whole room that needs decluttering – and blitz it! A clear space leads to a clearer mind.

Listen to the birds. Swap Twitter for actual tweeting. Birdsong has been shown to have a positive effect on mood. Plus you'll have the added benefits of connecting with nature.

Set up a playlist. It's well established that music can increase happiness and reduce anxiety, so put your favourite tunes into a playlist for an instantly clickable mood-booster.

39

Have a laugh. The saying "laughter is the best medicine" isn't far off the mark. Laughter increases the mood-enhancing chemical dopamine. Whether it's watching a comedy, clowning around with the kids or a night out with your besties, do something that makes you giggle.

Hug someone. Hugging releases the 'love hormone' oxytocin, which generates a warm, fuzzy feeling and promotes a sense of well-being. It can even have long-term health benefits.

Watch a cat video. In one study, researchers found that people felt more energetic and positive after watching cat videos. Not a cat person? Dog videos are fine too.

Play Wordle. If you're a fan of the hit word game Wordle, you'll know the sense of satisfaction that's derived from working out the daily challenge. Solving puzzles delivers a quick shot of dopamine – the chemical associated with pleasure and reward. Or you could try a sudoku, a crossword or even an old-fashioned jigsaw.

Grab some rays. Sunshine gets the serotonin flowing, which helps to elevate your mood. And you'll be grabbing some vitamin D at the same time, which also plays a role in mental well-being.

Smile. Even if you don't feel like smiling, doing so can trick your brain into feeling happy. It's a worth a try.

Smell some lavender. Lavender is well known for its soothing properties, and this is backed by science. Studies show that molecules in the essential oil really can improve your mood and reduce anxiety by interacting with the nervous system. And it smells gorgeous too.

Chew gum. As strange as it sounds, chewing gum has been found to alleviate poor mood and lower the stress hormone cortisol.

Tick one thing off your to-do list. It's easy to put off the chores we don't enjoy – the bill that needs paying, the form that needs filling, the floor that needs cleaning – but the feeling of getting something out of the way is better than the feeling of it hanging over us.

Relax your shoulders. If you have a habit of wearing your shoulders around your ears, let them drop and feel the tension slip away.

POSITIVITY AND SOCIAL MEDIA

Many of us spend more time than we'd like to admit, or perhaps than we even realize, glued to our phones, tablets and laptops.

Technology has revolutionized our lives, and there are many advantages to being plugged-in: we can communicate with friends and family, work from home, have our groceries delivered and find the answer to just about any question in the universe. However, there are plenty of downsides too, especially when it comes to social media.

There is simply no comparison: virtual interaction does not have the same benefit for our overall happiness as real interaction with other humans. What's more, if we're not careful, social media can have a seriously destructive effect on our real lives. Many studies have found a strong link between heavy social media use and an increased risk of depression, anxiety, self-harm, loneliness and even suicidal thoughts.

It's all too easy to scroll through other people's feeds, seemingly filled with success after success, blessing after blessing, and feel like our own lives are empty and bland in comparison, or that we are simply not enough. And even though we know that most people only post the edited highlights, this can have a terrible impact on our well-being. The good news is that by taking a step back from the noisy, unregulated world of the internet, we can seriously improve our mental health, our productivity, our ability to connect deeply with others, and ultimately, our happiness. Here are some actions to help you take back control.

Quit doomscrolling. There are many terrible things going on in the world. However, excessive doomscrolling, or mindlessly scrolling through negative news articles and social media posts, is unlikely to help solve them. On the contrary, doomscrolling distracts you from your own thoughts and feelings, increases anxiety and can damage overall well-being. While we need the news to help us grasp the world outside our own experience, it's important to be selective. Stick to balanced, independent sources of information and avoid clickbait and sensational news sites, or read a daily summary of the news instead. If you catch yourself inadvertently doomscrolling, make a point of logging off or doing something else.

Choose quality over quantity. Social media is littered with inane tweets and endless time-wasting posts that force you to read them just by being there. Spend some time going through the list of people you follow and delete those who sap your time and energy. Reserve your valuable headspace for people you actually care about or who have something interesting or useful to say.

Have a digital detox. If your relationship with social media has become a little toxic, then try a temporary separation. You may be surprised to find that things look a whole lot brighter after a period of abstinence.

Go old school. The trouble with phones is that we rely on them for so much more than making phone calls and sending texts. Besides communication devices, they are also cameras, watches, diaries, payment devices and so much more. While this is great for convenience (until you leave it on the train or drop it down a drain!) there is the constant temptation to check in with Facebook. Why not invest in a watch, a notebook and even a camera to help create a bit of distance.

Set a time limit. This is a simple one. Give yourself a time limit of, say, 20 minutes to scroll through Instagram or Twitter, then stop. Set an alarm to prevent you from going over and, if necessary, line up other tasks or engagements to help lure you away.

Pick a favourite. Many of us spread ourselves between a multitude of social media platforms – from Snapchat and TikTok to Instagram, Facebook and Pinterest. Ask yourself if you really need to be on all these sites. If not, pick one or two and delete the rest.

Make a pledge. Just as we need time away from work to unwind and focus on other things, we also need time away from social media too. One way to do this is to pledge to go screen-free every Sunday, then focus on all the other things you can do instead, even if it's just going for a tech-free walk. Things will soon start to look better when you do.

'Don't let the noise of others' opinions drown out your own inner voice. And most important, have the courage to follow your heart and intuition.'

Steve Jobs

ALL YOU NEED IS LOVE

We all need love in our lives. Supportive relationships are fundamental to our happiness and even our long-term health. But for this to happen, we first need to love ourselves.

Loving yourself has nothing to do with being vain or selfish, and everything to do with self-compassion. It simply means treating yourself with the same kindness, patience and understanding as you would treat someone you care about, especially someone going through a difficult time.

Being compassionate towards yourself will help you to live a more contented and fulfilling life. It will empower you to cope with challenges and work through struggles. It will also help others to see you in a more positive light, since the view we hold of ourselves is the view we project to those around us.

WAYS TO BUILD SELF-COMPASSION

The relationship you have with yourself will last a lifetime. So, here are some ways to show yourself some love.

Accept all your emotions. While it's important to notice the good things in our lives, this doesn't mean ignoring things that are upsetting or challenging. Suffering is an inevitable and unavoidable part of life, and it's important to acknowledge when you are going through a hard time. All emotions are valid, and toxic positivity – which seeks to dismiss emotions that are considered to be negative or 'bad' – only makes things worse and can seriously damage your well-being. Recognizing when you feel

'If you don't love yourself, you cannot love others. You will not be able to love others. If you have no compassion for yourself then you are not able of developing compassion for others.'

Dalai Lama

unhappy is the starting point for working out why, and for finding a solution.

Embrace your imperfections. We all make mistakes, it's part of being human. An important part of self-compassion is learning to accept any personal failings and to forgive yourself when you mess up. You could even try to see the funny side.

Be an observer. When you experience difficult emotions, try to notice and accept them as if viewing them from the outside, instead of dwelling on them and internalizing them. Remind yourself that you are more than your emotions.

Stop comparing. Comparison is the enemy of happiness since measuring yourself against other people is a one-way ticket to feeling inadequate. Instead of focusing on other people's achievements and good fortune, look for things to celebrate in your own life.

Be available – for yourself. It's vital for our physical and mental health to set limits. Sometimes that means saying no to things we don't really want to do, or don't have the capacity for. A good place to start is to put a note on your email signature saying you don't reply to emails during evenings or weekends. This reminds others that you are not a commodity and that your time matters. And don't feel guilty about needing time off from the kids.

Nourish your body. It's so easy to fall into the trap of associating healthy eating with looking a certain 'socially acceptable' way. Try to move away from the idea of foods being 'good' or 'bad' and focus instead on how eating well can improve your energy levels, mood and immune system.

Make time for self-reflection. When we plough through life on autopilot, we run the risk of losing touch with our own needs and desires, so it's vital to check in with ourselves and make time for self-reflection. This is an important part of personal growth. A great way to do this is to keep a journal. You might find your thoughts and emotions make more sense in black and white (or when using a purple glitter gel pen).

Make a date with yourself. What are the activities in life that really bring you joy? The people? The experiences? Whether it's mad nights out or cosy evenings in, exploring remote coastal paths or visiting bustling cities, or simply hanging out with your favourite people, make time for these things. When you do stuff you love, everything else starts to look better too.

'How you love yourself is how you teach others to love you.'

Rupi Kaur

STAY CONNECTED

Now that you have established the importance of having a positive relationship with yourself, it's time to think about your relationships with the people around you. Human connection is everything, and having deep, trusting relationships is one of the cornerstones of mental health. Quite simply: life is better shared. So, it's no surprise to hear that the happiest people on earth are those with strong relationships.

Unfortunately, we aren't all blessed with large, loving families, perfect relationships or a gazillion friends that we've known since we left the womb. Relationships fall apart, families can be dysfunctional, people let us down and move away, and sometimes we lose the people we love. But that doesn't mean we can't be happy or regain happiness. We all need – and deserve – the comfort, joy, support and security that comes from having other people in our lives – whether that's the family you were born into or the family you choose for yourself.

WAYS TO BUILD BETTER RELATIONSHIPS

Swap social media for social opportunities.
Platforms like Zoom and Facetime were a lifesaver during the lockdowns, and they can still be useful, especially if you live miles away from friends and family. However, nothing can compete with real, human interaction, so why not move your online chat or quiz night to a real-life setting?

Be a good friend. Friends are good for your health – fact. Therefore, it's just as important to invest in friendships as it is in romantic relationships. Go out of your way to be there for your friends; make them feel special, let them know how important they are to you, take time out for them, show up for them. Although, if you don't feel they give anything back, it may be time to move on, or at least talk to them about it.

Find your tribe. Whatever you're into – whether it's running, cycling, surfing, cold water swimming, crochet or writing poetry – there will be others out there who share the same interests. The pleasure of doing something you love is even greater when you do it with others, so search for groups in your area and join them. Go out there and be brave; you could end up making new friends for life.

Try something new. Is there something you've always wanted to do? Or perhaps you feel like you need a new hobby or outlet in your life. Embarking on a new skill or activity with others is a brilliant way to build confidence and broaden your social horizons. For example, you could join a sports team or a local running group (even if you are new to running), enrol on an evening class, a photography course or join a book club.

Make a difference. You don't need to be a special kind of person to make a difference to others, you just need to be willing. Perhaps you could help out in a community centre, visit people in hospital or prison, or listen to children read at your local school. There are so many ways to help out and you will get so much back in return, not least a sense of being valued.

Break up with the sofa. We are all guilty of zoning out in front of Netflix, especially after a long day, but spending time with others is vital for positive well-being. It might feel like an effort sometimes, but the benefits will be worth it.

Say hi! Simply smiling at strangers and saying hello helps us to feel connected. And you never know the difference it might make to someone else's day too.

> '**There is no hope of joy except in human relations.**'
>
> **Antoine de Saint-Exupéry**

Be vulnerable. Allowing others to see the real you takes courage, honesty and communication, but it is key to strengthening your most meaningful relationships. It's OK to say you're not OK.

Focus on your nearest and dearest. When we are busy, it's often our closest relationships that suffer. So, arrange a date night, spend more time playing with your children or visit that family member you haven't seen for ages.

Cut ties that don't serve you. We all need people in our lives who lift us up and bring out our best. As for the rest, sometimes the only option is to let them go.

GLORIOUS GRATITUDE

You are probably already familiar with the word 'gratitude'. It's a term that's often waved around, but that doesn't mean it's just another fad. Gratitude is simply about making a conscious effort to notice and appreciate the things in our lives that bring us joy, especially the non-physical things.

Practising gratitude on a regular basis helps to shift our awareness from the negative to the positive. This helps to reduce the impact of stress and negative emotions, which, of course, improves our general outlook.

Studies show that expressing gratitude causes the brain to emit chemicals associated with well-being. Like other positive behaviours, it's most effective when it becomes a habit. One way to make gratitude part of your life is to keep a 'gratitude journal'. At the end of each day, make a note of three things – however tiny or insignificant they may seem – that brought you joy. Research shows that this is an effective way to increase long-term feelings of happiness and well-being.

Here are just some of the ways in which practising gratitude can help boost your physical and mental health.

- Better immunity.

- Improved sleep.

- A reduction in stress.

- Lower blood pressure.

- Great self-esteem.

- Less anxiety and depression.

- Healthier relationships.

'Gratitude blocks toxic emotions, such as envy, resentment, regret and depression, which can destroy our happiness.'

Robert Emmons

- A more hopeful outlook on life.

- A greater desire to adopt a healthier lifestyle.

- More positive emotions.

- Greater focus on the present moment.

LITTLE WAYS TO NURTURE GRATITUDE

- Name at least one person who lights up your life.

- Say thank you to that person for being a positive influence.

- Stop to notice the beauty of something you normally take for granted – a flower, a sunset, the way the rain dances on tarmac.

- Reflect on the amazing work your body does every day just to keep you alive.

- Acknowledge the little things in your life that bring you joy.

- Think of a place that brings you peace.

- Give thanks for something that makes your life easier.

- Spend a few moments reliving a happy memory.

- Each day, say out loud or write down five things for which you're grateful.

- Take a moment to appreciate something really delicious you've eaten recently.

- Think of a gift or small possession that brings you joy when you look at it, such as a photograph or something from your childhood.

THINGS WILL LOOK BETTER WITH KINDNESS

Like gratitude, 'kindness' is another word that frequently crops up in memes and on T-shirts. It's become so common that it's easy to forget how important it is.

When someone is kind to us, it helps us to see the world in a better light. But that's not all. When we do something kind for someone else, it increases our own feelings of confidence, self-worth and compassion.

Perhaps you're already familiar with the warm, fuzzy feeling that comes from helping someone in need, or knowing you've made even a small difference to someone else's life. That's because when you do something nice for someone else it triggers your brain to release dopamine, giving you a natural high. In other words, being kind doesn't just benefit the recipient, it can have a positive impact on your own mental health too. It's a win-win situation.

BE KIND, BOOST YOUR MIND

Kindness and happiness are closely linked. Have a go at some of these acts of kindness and notice how you feel.

- Phone a friend who is struggling with their relationship. Take the time to listen.

- If you know a parent who could use a break, offer to look after their kids for a while.

- Visit an elderly neighbour, or ask if they need any errands running.

- Ask someone who doesn't seem to know many people in the area to join you for a walk, a coffee, a drink or just a chat.

- Send flowers to someone you care about – just because.

- Pay someone a compliment and watch them glow.

- Bake a cake for someone as a surprise.

- Give blood.

- Donate items to your local food bank.

- If you are in a position to do so, offer a spare room to a refugee, or sign up to register your willingness.

- Say hello instead of just walking past.

- Support a new business (even if you could find the same products cheaper elsewhere).

- Say thank you to cleaners and refuse collectors – let them know they are valued.

'Carry out a random act of kindness, with no expectation of reward, safe in the knowledge that one day someone might do the same for you.'

Princess Diana

- Offer to walk someone's dog.

- Pass on clothes or books you no longer need to someone who might appreciate them.

- If you have children, pass on their outgrown clothes or toys to someone who could use them.

- If you can afford to do so, buy some groceries for someone who is struggling financially. If you think they might be embarrassed, say you were clearing out your cupboards and won't use them yourself.

- Write a positive review.

JUST SLOW DOWN

Do you ever feel like you are being swept along in a hurricane? In our 24/7, always-on-the-go society, it can be hard to catch your breath, let alone your thoughts.

Many of us race through life with a squillion things to do, heads down, hands over ears, faster and faster, as the noise in our brains becomes louder and louder, and it becomes harder and harder to see where we're going, or where we want to go, or even who we really are.

The upshot is that we end up feeling anxious, frazzled, out of control and overwhelmed by a list of obligations and commitments. And if we're not careful, we can crash and burn. Which isn't exactly the ideal position to be in when it comes to looking on the bright side.

But we can turn down the volume. We can replace the inner cacophony with inner peace. We. Can. Slow. Down.

One way to do this is through mindfulness. Originating in meditation, mindfulness is a gentle way of focusing your mind and centring yourself in the present moment. The idea is to bring your awareness to your surroundings and your senses – what you see, what you feel, what you taste, what you smell – in order to draw your attention away from negative or distracting thoughts. This can help you to feel calmer and more grounded, which, in time, can lead to a more positive outlook on life.

Developing the ability to calm your thoughts also has a protective effect on well-being, since when challenging situations come along, as they invariably will, you will feel more in control and less overwhelmed. Mindfulness can take a bit of practice. To start with, you might find your mind keeps wandering: jumping ahead to the future, or back to the past, or getting tangled up in negative thoughts. If this happens, don't worry. Just notice these thoughts and accept that they are nothing more than mental events that come and go like clouds in the sky.

MINDFUL BREATHING

This simple, calming, breathing exercise provides a gentle introduction to mindfulness.

- Sitting comfortably, or lying on your back, let your arms and hands relax. Close your eyes if you like.

- Starting with your forehead – then moving on to your neck, shoulders, and so on, until you get to your toes – focus your attention on your body. Notice any areas of tension and gently try to let them go.

- Now bring your attention to your breathing. Don't try to change it, just notice how your chest rises and falls as you inhale and exhale. Pay attention to the way it feels.

- Don't worry if your mind wanders and you find yourself thinking about something other than your breathing, just calmly bring your attention back to the sensation of your breath going in and out.

- Try to focus on your breathing for around five minutes. Then slowly return your attention to the rest of your body, then to your surroundings, before carrying on with your day, calm and alert.

EVERYDAY MINDFULNESS

The beauty of mindfulness is that you can use it as you go about your daily life. It's amazing how often we just go through the motions, accompanied by the constant buzzing of our phones, without ever really noticing what's around us. However, by inviting a more conscious approach to our everyday activities, mindfulness offers a welcome antidote to the frenzied nature of modern living. You can try to be mindful at home, at work, while eating, or even while doing the chores. Here are a few suggestions.

- When you are hanging out the washing, or folding it away, breathe in the freshly laundered scent, run your fingers over the fabric, noticing the different textures.

'Happiness is when what you think, what you say, and what you do are in harmony.'

Mahatma Gandhi

- When you get into bed, feel the coolness of the sheets against your skin, notice the smoothness of your pillow against your cheek.

- Take a mindful stroll, paying attention to your surroundings. Walking is a great opportunity to be mindful.

- When you are outdoors, open your senses to the elements; feel the caress of the sun, wind or rain on your skin.

- The next time you drink a coffee, resist the urge to gulp it down on the run, but savour every molecule: the rich aroma, the warmth of the mug in your hand, the taste, the after-taste. Permit yourself a few minutes just to sit down and enjoy it before continuing with your day.

CUT YOURSELF SOME SLACK

There is so much pressure in society to be busy and productive that we often feel guilty when we are *not* constantly on the go, as if there is a sense of shame and stigma in taking time out. As a result, it's easy to associate giving ourselves a much-needed break with being lazy – or being perceived by others to be lazy.

Perhaps you don't feel worthy of taking time off, or are worried that you will fall behind or miss out. Or perhaps being constantly 'up to your eyes in it' is your way of proving to yourself – and others – that you are valuable, important and needed. But here's the thing: you are all of these things and more, and you don't need to be relentlessly, exhaustingly busy to prove it.

Ironically, even activities that are supposed to benefit our well-being, such as yoga or going to the gym, can become just another thing on our to-do list. And when 'chilling out' becomes an effort, that too can become another source of stress. If you feel like you have too many balls in the air – whether it's work, family, caring for elderly relatives, or even trying to keep up with a punishing personal training schedule – there is no shame in lowering your standards. In fact, things will look much better when you do. Of course, any changes you make will depend on your unique situation, but here are some suggestions.

Have one night off a week. If you normally cook from scratch, choose at least one night a week where you don't bother and buy something ready-made. It doesn't have to be processed or unhealthy; something like fresh soup is effortless and nutritious.

Ask for help. If you're drowning in chores, ask family members to help. If you can afford to, consider taking on a cleaner.

Avoid perfectionism. Whether it's helping the kids construct a model of the Titanic, baking cakes for a cake sale or writing a mammoth report, remember your best is good enough.

Flex your right to DNA. That's not the stuff in cells, but your right to Do Not Attend. Whether it's after-work drinks, a wedding, christening or family obligation you don't really want to go to, weigh up the cost to your well-being versus the cost of being present. If it's going to put your well-being in the red, politely decline.

Confront your inner neat freak. Do you really need to wash the bedding or the floors every week? Is ironing really necessary? Sometimes there really is no harm in letting things slip. A bit of dirt is good for the immune system anyway!

'The day she let go of the things that were weighing her down was the day she began to shine the brightest.'

Katrina Mayer

Simplify your life. Multitasking and stress go hand in hand, so try to avoid doing three things with one hand and focus on doing one thing with both hands. It may feel counter-productive but you will feel less overwhelmed, and you will end up with better results.

'Be happy in the moment, that's enough. Each moment is all we need, not more.'

Mother Teresa

THE SWEETNESS OF NOTHING

There is well-loved phrase in Italian, *il dolce far niente*, which translates as 'how sweet it is to do nothing'. Yet when was the last time you did absolutely nothing? In our goal-driven, work-mad society, many of us rarely, if ever, take a well-deserved pause. Even our leisure time has to be 'improving', as if every waking minute needs to serve a purpose.

In contrast, *il dolce far niente* is literally the art of doing nothing and enjoying it. And no, that doesn't mean scrolling through social media or zoning out in front of the TV. It's about letting time pass by and allowing your thoughts to take over. In this simple, blissful state, all that matters is existing: no pressure, no activities, no worries, just the delicious, guilt-free pleasure of being idle. Yes, idle!

The idea of 'wasting time' might sound completely alien and incompatible with modern life. It might even sound pointless. But there is much to be gained from briefly switching off. It provides an opportunity for the mind and body to recalibrate, clearing the way for creativity, thoughts and ideas to wander in.

LITTLE MOMENTS OF
IL DOLCE FAR NIENTE

Why not permit yourself a few moments to just be,
while the world keeps turning. Here are some ideas to get
you started.

- Allow yourself to get lost in daydream.

- Gaze out of the window.

- Lie on a blanket under the stars.

- Observe the clouds.

- Slump into a beanbag in your favourite room.

- Sit down with a glass of wine.

- Sit outside a café and watch the world go by.

- While away the time with a close friend.

- Sunbathe.

- Stop and rest for a few minutes on a park bench.

FINDING MEANING AND VALUE

Having meaning in our lives helps us to feel happy and fulfilled. Studies show that people who feel that their lives are meaningful tend to experience more positive emotions and feel better about the future.

Having a sense of meaning in life also helps us to be more resilient, since believing in ourselves and our place in the world gives us the strength to face challenges and work through adversity.

The way we find and experience meaning can differ from person to person, but essentially it's about feeling connected to something more than just than ourselves. We are all connected to the world around us in all sorts of ways, from the colleagues we work with, to the people we sit next to on the bus, from the politicians we vote for, to the healthcare professionals that look after us, to the animals that share our environment and the bees that pollinate our food. Reflecting on the ways in which we are connected to others, and how we can positively interact with these connections, is just one step towards finding meaning in life. Here are some more.

Be authentic. Developing an understanding of who you really are, and living in a way that feels genuine and sincere, is key to a happy and meaningful life. It can be hard not to succumb to the pressure to fit in or follow the crowd, but true, lasting happiness comes from being yourself.

Be guided by your values. Sometimes we do things because we feel we 'should' or because someone else tells us we should, not because we really want to. However, for an activity to be truly meaningful, it must

'The privilege of a lifetime is to become who you truly are.'

C. G. Jung

sit comfortably with your own principles. When our actions conflict with our values, this can leave us feeling uncomfortable and unfulfilled.

Follow your heart. What do you really want to do in life? What do you most desire? Whether it's having children, writing a novel or climbing mountains, pursue the projects that are the most important to you. These are the ones that will bring the most fulfilment.

'The only thing that will make you happy is being happy with who you are, and not who people think you are.'

Goldie Hawn

Engage in worthwhile activities. If you don't derive much satisfaction from your job (or even if you do), look for meaningful opportunities outside of work, such as volunteering, community projects or prioritizing family time. Or simply spend an hour or two a week on a hobby that is important to you.

Explore your spiritual side. Whether it's through prayer, worship, meditation or nature, connecting with something that feels beyond yourself can lead to a deep sense of peace of mind.

CARRY ON LEARNING

Learning isn't just for school, it's a lifelong process. As adults, learning a new skill or developing a new hobby is a fantastic way to boost well-being and positivity. It boosts confidence, self-esteem, creativity, curiosity and resilience, and give us a huge sense of satisfaction and accomplishment. Whether you are nine or 90, learning doesn't just sharpen your brain, it also contributes to a brighter outlook on life.

AND DON'T GIVE UP...

Learning new skills isn't always easy, especially if you haven't challenged yourself for a while. Fortunately, research shows the brain is like a muscle: the more you use it, the more it changes and grows. This is because when we develop new skills and absorb new information, the connections between neurons multiply and get stronger. Scientists call this 'neuroplasticity', and it means there is nothing stopping you from mastering a new skill except your own mindset.

There are two types of mindsets: fixed and growth. People with a fixed mindset tend to give up if they don't get something right straight away, since they don't believe they can improve or change their abilities. Conversely, people with a growth mindset believe that with practice, or by trying a different approach, they can get better. They know that mistakes are part of the learning process

'Optimism is the faith that leads to achievement. Nothing can be done without hope and confidence.'

Helen Keller

... UNTIL YOU FIND YOUR FLOW

'Flow' is that magical state of being that happens when you become so absorbed in something that you lose track of time and place. And in this state, there is no room left for worries or negative thoughts. Flow occurs when we are fully engaged in something that is both challenging (but not impossible) and deeply enjoyable. The peace of mind and sense of fulfilment derived from reaching a state of flow is a great way to boost your well-being. It's like discovering a natural antidepressant! And when you return to your normal activities, you will be in a more positive state of mind.

Unfortunately, our hectic lives mean there are so many things we *need* to do that it can be hard to make time for the things we really *want* to do. Use these tips to help create space for flow.

- Reflect on the things you would love to be good at, or an interest you would love to explore. What one thing have you always wanted to try? Try to find something that requires some skill and takes you just outside your comfort zone. For example, it could be painting, gardening, learning to crochet or play an instrument.

- Find a regular time that you can set aside to engage in your chosen activity. Then do your best to stick to it.

- Choose a place where you won't be distracted by children or phones. Let others know this is 'your time'.

- Make finding time for flow a part of your routine. Make it something you look forward to, and feel your well-being soar.

BEYOND OURSELVES: MAKING A DIFFERENCE IN THE WORLD

It can be hard to feel positive when confronted with the many issues going on in the world. From wars and refugees to plastic pollution, carbon emissions and climate change, there is much to be concerned about. And in the face of such enormous, indisputable challenges, it's natural to feel a sense of sadness and despair.

However, we can use these feelings for good. Instead of feeling hopeless and powerless, we can turn sorrow and indignation into action.

Although our actions may seem small and insignificant on an individual level, on a collective level they can literally change the world. What's more, when we become part of the solution, this helps us to feel more positive, connected and empowered, boosting our own well-being as well as that of the planet.

You are probably already ahead of the game when it comes to using refillable water bottles, reusable shopping bags and putting out the recycling. Here are some more ideas you could adopt for a brighter future and a brighter today.

Go wild for flowers. Packets of wildflower seed mixes are cheap and readily available in shops and online. They are a brilliant way of creating a mini haven for insects like bees, butterflies and moths, which are crucial for pollination and biodiversity. All you need is a small patch of earth (a few pots or a window box will do if you don't have any outdoor space), then simply scatter the seed and wait for the flowers to appear.

Get muddy. Growing even a little of what you eat reduces waste, lowers your carbon footprint, encourages wildlife and reduces the use of harmful pesticides or fertilizers. Plus, you'll have delicious, fresh food at your fingertips. You don't even need a garden; herbs and salad leaves will grow brilliantly on a kitchen windowsill, while many crops, like tomatoes, strawberries and beans, are perfect for pots and patio containers. If you are lucky enough to have a garden, then the sky's your limit. If you have time, you could think about taking on an allotment or getting involved with a community garden. What's more, gardening is hugely beneficial for mental health, helping to boost mood while reducing symptoms of depression, anxiety and stress.

Buy rubbish. From swimwear and trainers to soft furnishings and rucksacks, many forward-thinking companies have found ways to turn trash into treasure, creating beautiful products from recycled plastic and ocean waste. Supporting these brands boosts small businesses and reduces your impact on the planet.

Walk it off. Not only is walking great for your physical and mental health, it's completely free and comes at zero cost to the environment. Remember how much you appreciated getting outside during lockdown? Keep those steps going.

Embrace slow fashion. The fashion industry has become a parasite on the environment. Cotton production requires vast quantities of water and uses more pesticides than any other crop in the world. Meanwhile, synthetic fabrics fill the oceans with microplastics, contributing to the destruction of marine life. You can help put an end to this by steering clear of fast fashion and focusing on quality rather than quantity, including items made from more sustainable fabrics like bamboo. Or why not have fun hunting for second-hand gems in charity shops or online?

Put your money where your heart is. As a consumer, you have a choice about which companies you use. Check out where banks and energy companies invest your money and only invest in those that are green and ethical.

Save your energy. Conserving energy saves money and helps lower your carbon footprint. There are all sorts of actions you can take, including switching to energy-saving bulbs, turning down the heating, batch cooking when the oven is on, turning off appliances when you're not using them, turning down the thermostat, washing at lower temperatures, hanging clothes outside to dry instead of using a tumble dryer, and insulating your home.

Plant trees as you search online. Ecosia is the search engine that plants trees. Every search generates income through search ads, and Ecosia uses this income to plant trees. The company dedicates 100 per cent of its profits to climate action, with at least 80 per cent going towards tree-planting projects. And it's completely free to install!

AND FINALLY

You never know what life will throw your way. We all go through periods when it's hard to see the sun for the clouds, or when life just feels like an uphill struggle. However, things really can look better when we know where, or how, to look. We can't always change our circumstances – at least not overnight – but we can change the way we think, for a happier today and a happier tomorrow.

Positivity isn't determined by what we have on the outside but by what we have on the inside. Positive people aren't immune from stress and suffering; however, they strive to navigate tough times with resilience and optimism. They treasure small moments of joy instead of replaying negative thoughts and emotions. And even when times are hard, they believe that better days are coming.

Hopefully, this book has inspired you to keep searching for the silver linings and to super-charge your life with gratitude, kindness and self-compassion. Our journey on this earth may not always go in the direction we'd like, but by changing the way we think, searching for the good, and working on the relationships we have with others and ourselves, we can all experience a deeper sense of inner contentment. And when that happens, things really will look better. Because, as each new day proves, even the darkest night is always followed by morning.

"For there is always light,
If only we're brave enough to see it,
If only we're brave enough to be it."

Amanda Gorman